# Benjamin Franklin

Jennifer Strand

**abdopublishing.com**

Published by Abdo Zoom™, PO Box 398166, Minneapolis, Minnesota 55439. Copyright © 2017 by Abdo Consulting Group, Inc. International copyrights reserved in all countries. No part of this book may be reproduced in any form without written permission from the publisher. Abdo Zoom™ is a trademark and logo of Abdo Consulting Group, Inc.

Printed in the United States of America, North Mankato, Minnesota
072016
092016

Cover Photo: Corbis
Interior Photos: Corbis, 1; Georgios Kollidas/Shutterstock Images, 5; North Wind Picture Archives, 6, 7, 8, 9, 10, 14, 15, 18; Everett Historical/Shutterstock Images, 10–11, 12, 16; Joseph-Siffrède Duplessis/Library of Congress, 13; David Sucsy/iStockphoto, 16–17

Editor: Emily Temple
Series Designer: Madeline Berger
Art Direction: Dorothy Toth

**Publisher's Cataloging-in-Publication Data**
Names: Strand, Jennifer, author.
Title: Benjamin Franklin / by Jennifer Strand.
Description: Minneapolis, MN : Abdo Zoom, [2017] | Series: Incredible inventors
    | Includes bibliographical references and index.
Identifiers: LCCN 2016941397 | ISBN 9781680792287 (lib. bdg.) |
    ISBN 9781680793963 (ebook) | 9781680794854 (Read-to-me ebook)
Subjects: LCSH: Franklin, Benjamin, 1706-1790--Juvenile literature. | Statesmen-
    -United States--Biography--Juvenile literature. | Scientists--United States--
    Biography--Juvenile literature. | Inventors--United States--Biography--
    Juvenile literature. | Printers--United States--Biography--Juvenile literature.
Classification: DDC 973.3/092 [B]--dc23
LC record available at http://lccn.loc.gov/2016941397

# Table of Contents

# Introduction

Benjamin Franklin was a writer and inventor. He was also a scientist. He helped the United States become a country.

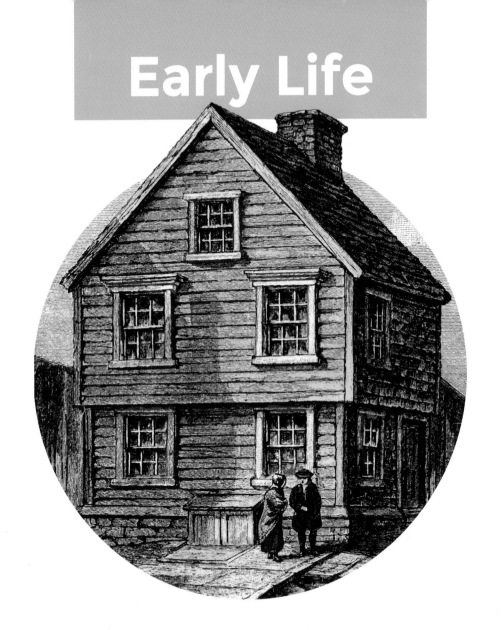

Benjamin was born on
January 17, 1706.

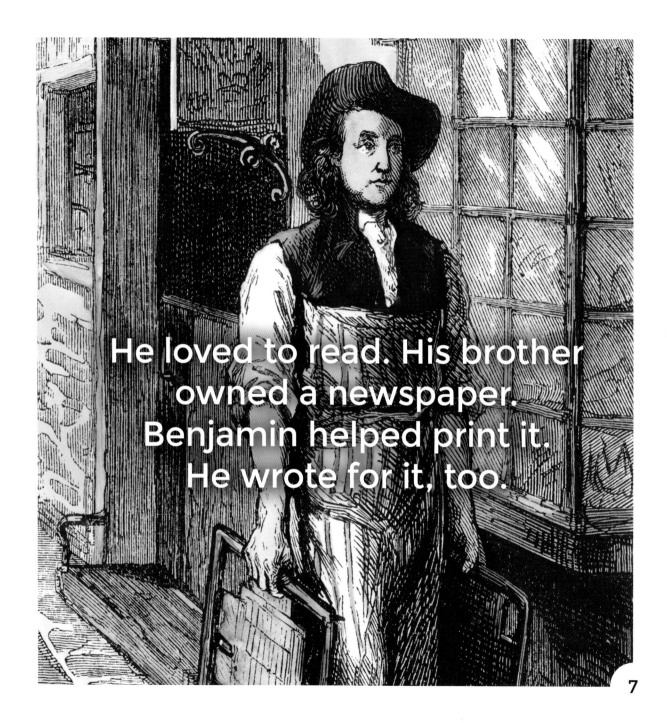

He loved to read. His brother owned a newspaper. Benjamin helped print it. He wrote for it, too.

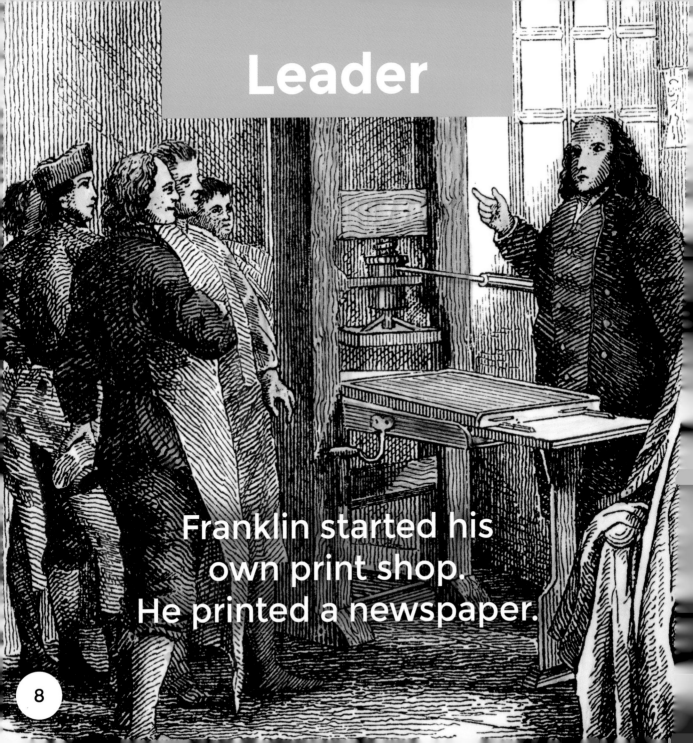

# Leader

Franklin started his
own print shop.
He printed a newspaper.

He made an **almanac**, too.
It had funny sayings. Some
of them became famous.

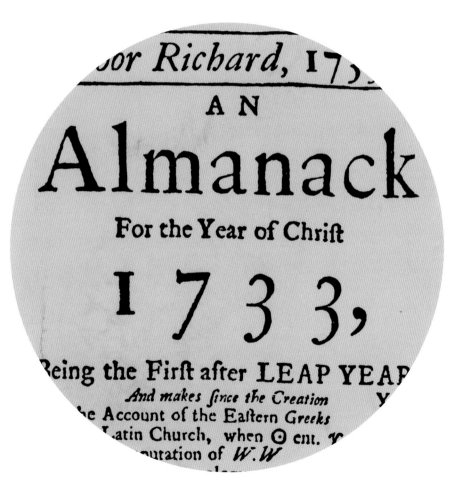

Franklin studied science.
He did **experiments**.

He showed that lightning was electricity. He also invented things.

# History Maker

The American **colonies** wanted to be free from Britain. Franklin tried to keep peace. But war broke out.

12

Franklin supported
the colonies. He got the
French to help them fight.

Franklin helped create the **Declaration of Independence**. The colonies soon became free.

He worked on the
US Constitution.

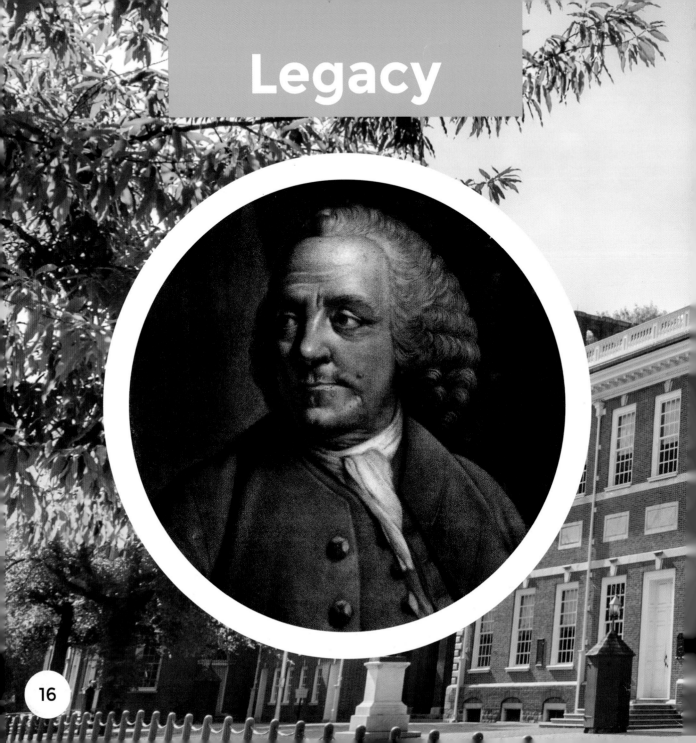

# Legacy

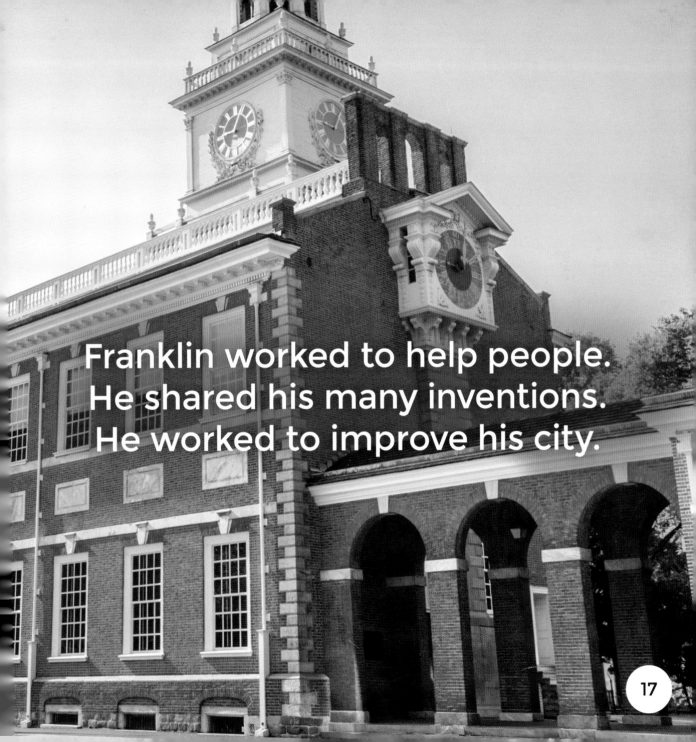

Franklin worked to help people.
He shared his many inventions.
He worked to improve his city.

Franklin became very famous.
On April 17, 1790, he died.

Many people still read his writings. Sayings from his almanac are common today, too.

# Benjamin Franklin

**Born:** January 17, 1706

**Birthplace:** Boston, Massachusetts

**Wife:** Deborah Read Rogers

**Known For:** Franklin helped the United States become a country. He was also an inventor.

**Died:** April 17, 1790

# Key Dates

**1706:** Benjamin Franklin is born on January 17.

**1732:** Franklin begins publishing *Poor Richard's Almanack*.

**1752:** Franklin does an experiment with a kite to study lightning and electricity.

**1757:** Franklin travels to England to try and keep peace.

**1776:** Franklin helps write the Declaration of Independence.

**1790:** Franklin dies on April 17.

# Glossary

**almanac** - a book with facts and stories about a given year.

**colony** - a new settlement that is connected to a faraway country.

**Constitution** - the most basic laws that govern the United States.

**Declaration of Independence** - the document that said the American colonies were free from Great Britain.

**experiment** - a scientific test.

# Booklinks

For more information
on **Benjamin Franklin**, please visit
booklinks.abdopublishing.com

**Z○○m** In on Biographies!

Learn even more with the Abdo Zoom
Biographies database. Check out
**abdozoom.com** for more information.

# Index